THE WONDERFUL STORY OF CREATION

Written and illustrated by

Magdalena Kim, FSP

Pauline
BOOKS & MEDIA
Boston

Library of Congress Cataloging-in-Publication Data

Kim, Magdalena.
  [Who is the Mother of the Earth?]
  The wonderful story of creation / written and illustrated by Magdalena Kim ; translated by Gratia Chang ; edited and adapted by Patricia Edward Jablonski.
      p. cm.
Originally published: Who is the Mother of the Earth? Seoul, Korea : Daughters of St. Paul, 1993.
  ISBN 0-8198-8300-X (pbk.)
  1. Creation—Juvenile literature. 2. Bible stories, English—O.T.—Genesis.
[1. Creation. 2. Bible stories—O.T. Genesis.] I. Jablonski, Patricia E. II. Title.
  BS651 .K48 2001
  233'.11—dc21
                          2001000469

Translated from the Korean by Gratia Chang, FSP

Edited and adapted by Patricia Edward Jablonski, FSP

Original edition title: *Who is the Mother of the Earth?*

Copyright © 1993, Daughters of St. Paul / Korea

Published by Pauline, 103 Mia-9dong Kangbuk-gu, 142-704 Seoul, Korea.
All rights reserved.

English edition copyright © 2001, Daughters of St. Paul / U.S.A.

Illustrations copyright © 1993, Daughters of St. Paul / Korea

Printed and published in the U.S.A. by Pauline Books & Media, 50 Saint Pauls Avenue, Boston, MA 02130-3491.

www. pauline.org

Pauline Books & Media is the publishing house of the Daughters of St. Paul, an international congregation of women religious serving the Church with the communications media.

1 2 3 4 5 6   06 05 04 03 02 01

A long, long time ago, the Earth was a small, dark planet. One day, it began to wriggle in excitement.

"What's happening?" one little angel wondered.

"What is God doing?" a second little angel asked.

6

"It seems as if the Earth is breathing!"

"Do you see that light God is making? It's so pretty!"

The two little angels flapped their wings in joy.

When the light reached the Earth, the Earth sparkled with a beautiful green color. God smiled and said, "It looks good!"

Above the green Earth, God then made the blue sky with its fluffy white clouds.

"I'd like to sleep on a cloud," said one little angel with a yawn.

"So would I!" answered the other.

The mischievous little angels flew in and out of the clouds as the clouds playfully tried to run away.

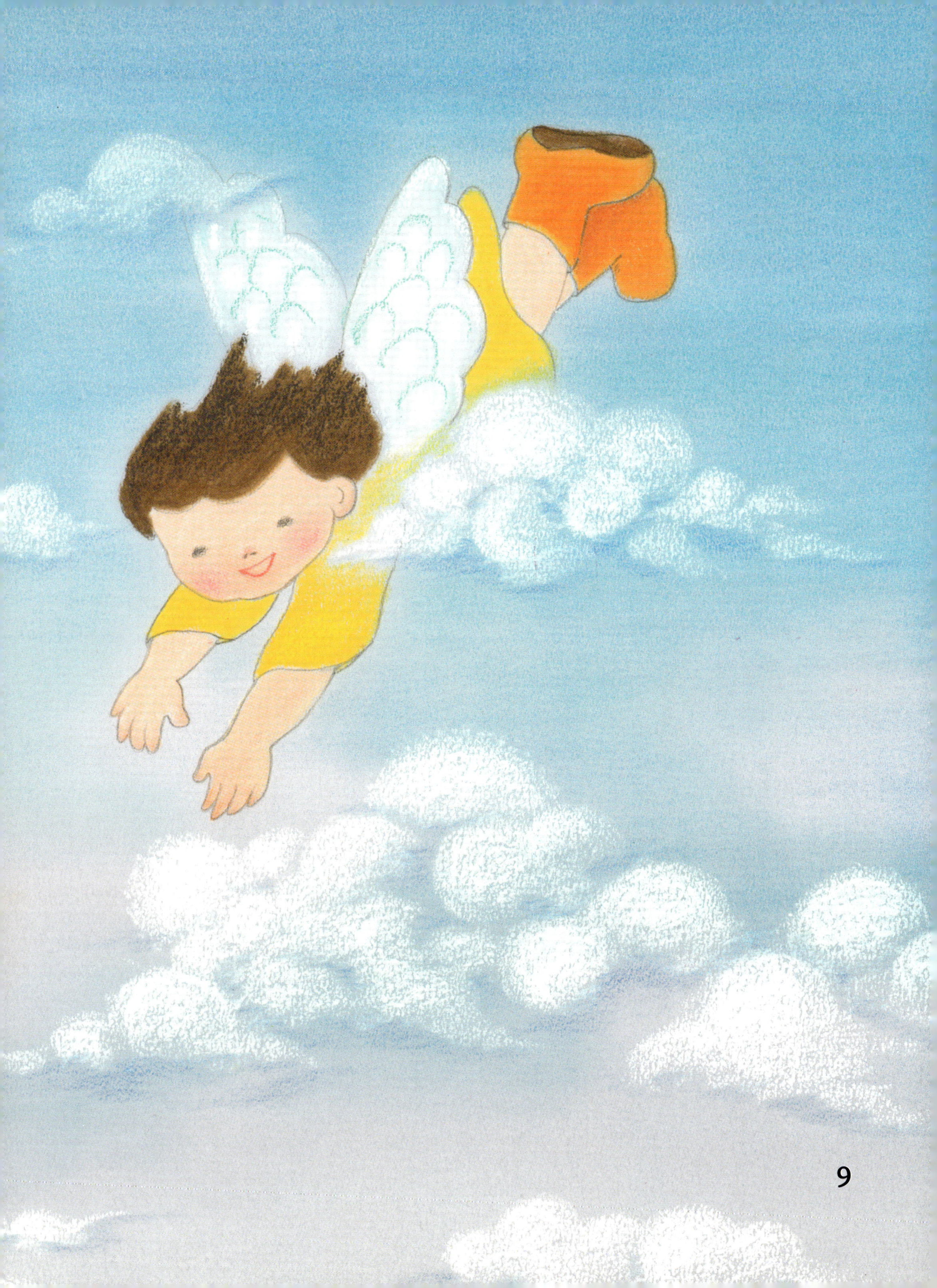

Plop. Plop. Plop. Drops of rain began to fall from the sky. Plop. Plop. Plop. Soon the raindrops became a huge puddle of water.

"Let's call this water the ocean," God said.

11

When all the water came together, some of the Earth became brown dirt. The dirt was waiting for God's word.

"Come up, green grass!" God said. "Grow, pretty flowers! Make the Earth happy!"

Up through the dirt popped shiny, green grass.

Up came red and yellow, white and blue flowers. The little angels couldn't believe what they were seeing. "It's almost as beautiful as heaven!" they cried in surprise.

Day after day wonderful things kept happening on the Earth.

"God, what will you make today?" asked one of the little angels.

"Look and see!" said God. "Let every kind of fruit tree be born!"

The Earth squirmed and shook. Big, strong trees came up through the dirt. Delicious fruit hung on their branches.

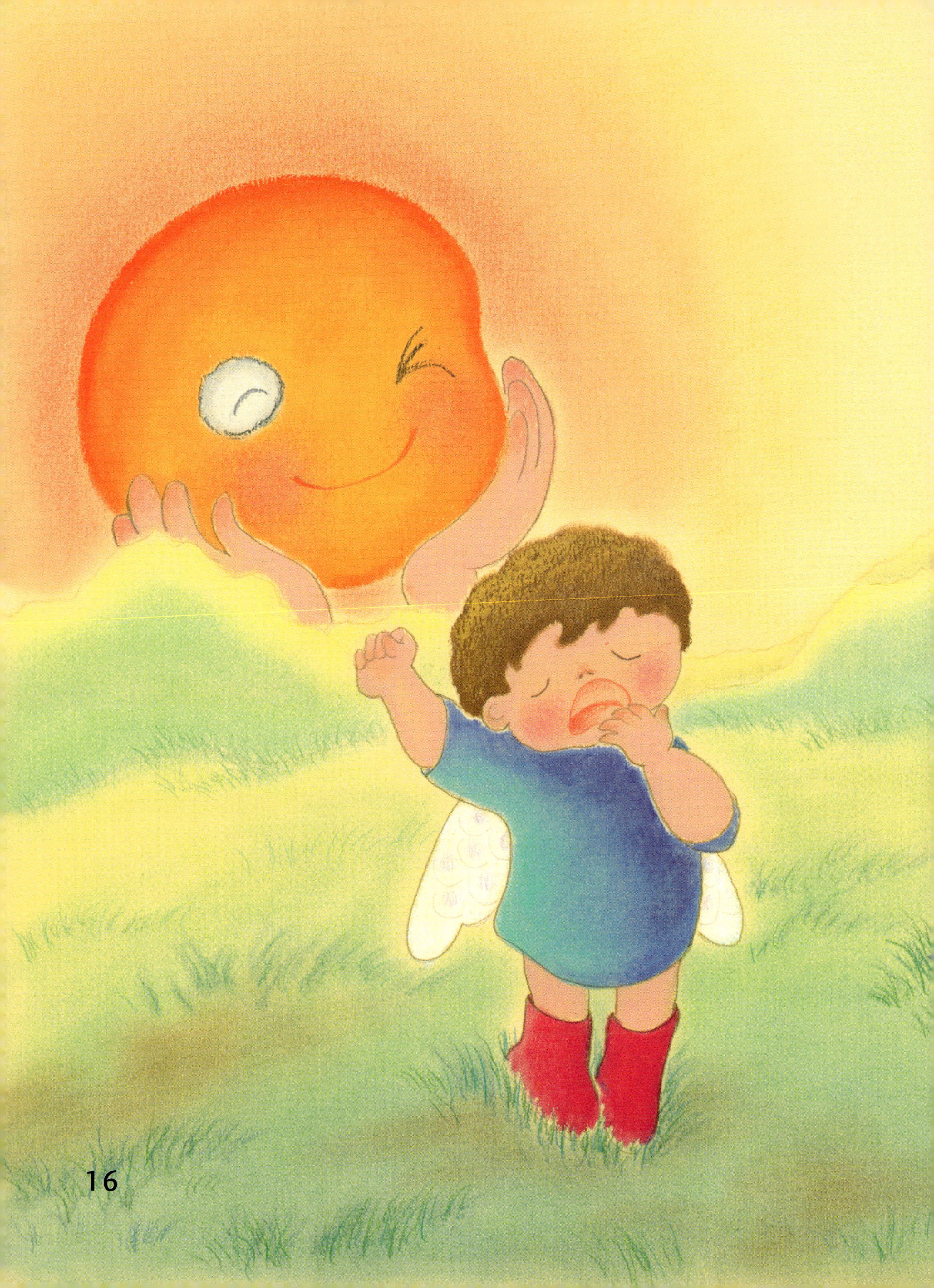

The little angels were very happy with everything they saw. But they had one important question. "God, what will happen if the light goes away?" they asked.

"You don't have to worry about that," God kindly answered. Then he said, "Let the sun be born!" And the sun was born.

Soon the little angels began to worry again. "You're too hot!" they told the sun. "Go away. You might burn the Earth!"

"No," God told the angels. "The sun will only appear during the day. At night, the stars and the moon will watch over the Earth. The sun, the moon and the stars will be the Earth's friends."

And so God made the moon and the stars, too.

19

Then the little angels said, "The Earth is filled with many things, but the water looks bored."

"I have more to do," God answered. "Just watch and see! Ocean, be filled with many fish, shells and plants!"

Now the deep ocean had become as beautiful as the Earth.

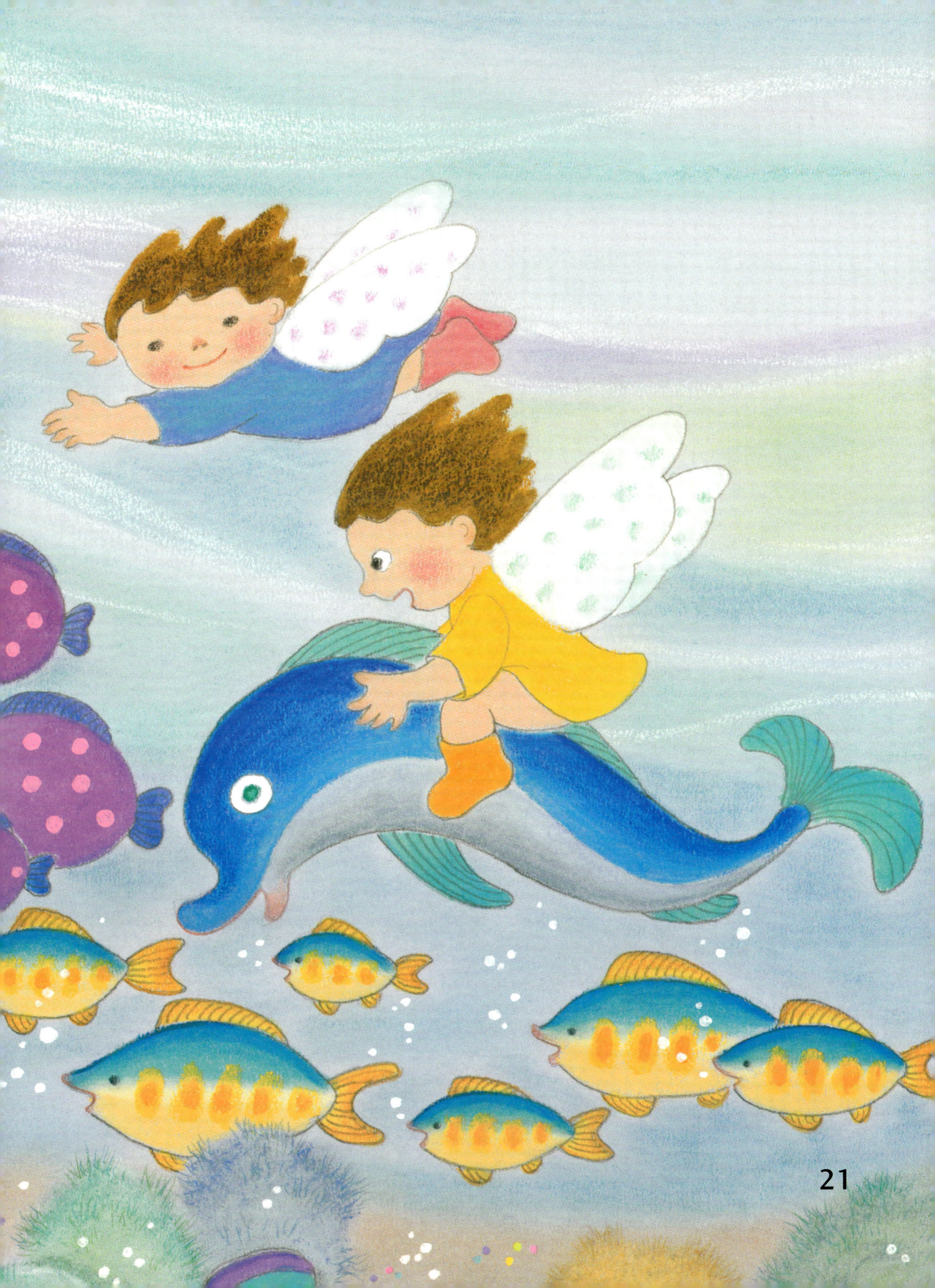

Next God said,
"I give the Earth flying
friends. Birds, be born!"

Suddenly the sky was filled with
all kinds of birds making happy
chirping sounds.
"Flying friends, be quiet!" the little
angels said with a smile.

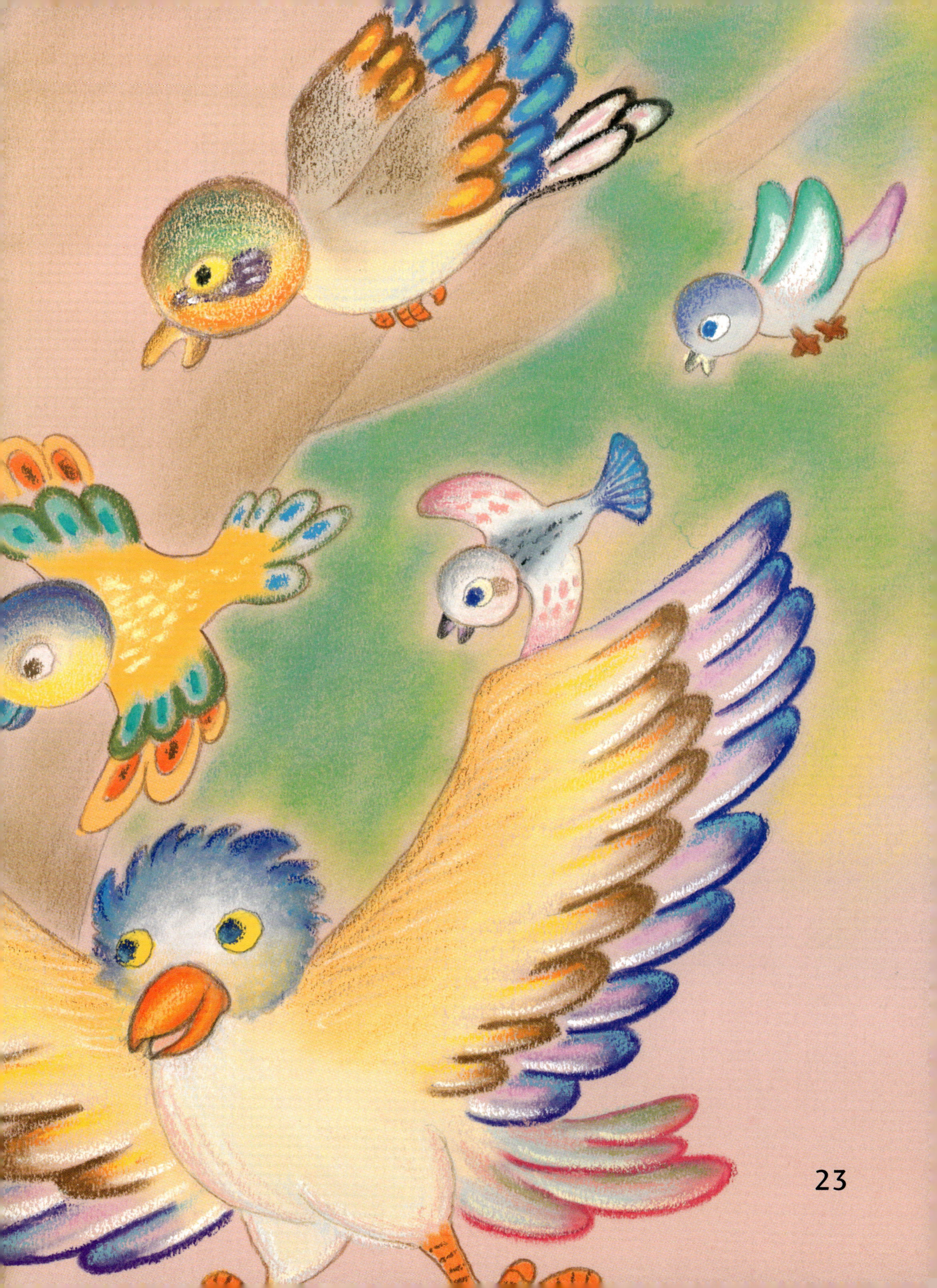

24

"Just look at those animals!" giggled one of the angels, pointing at a pig and a cow. "They have such big bottoms!"

"How talented God is!" said the other angel. "He can make so many different creatures, both big and small."

"Look there!" exclaimed the first little angel. "Even though they have many legs, those tiny bugs can't walk too far. But their wings shine like a rainbow!"

The other little angel jumped onto the elephant's back.

"Come down!" the elephant shouted, trying to shake him off. "Don't you know that I'm still just a baby?"

"God, are you finished with your work yet?" the little angels finally asked.

"I have one more very special thing to do," God answered. "Maybe it will surprise you. Close your eyes. Now open them!"

"Wow!" the angels exclaimed. "These new creatures look so nice!"

"Yes," God said. "They are my own son and daughter. They are the very first people to live on the Earth. They are the creatures I love the most!"

30

This is the story of how God created our wonderful world. God has put us, his sons and daughters, in charge of all the beautiful things he has made. Let's take good care of one another and of all God's creation!

Pauline
BOOKS & MEDIA

The Daughters of St. Paul operate book and media centers at the following addresses. Visit, call or write the one nearest you today, or find us on the World Wide Web, www.pauline.org

CALIFORNIA
3908 Sepulveda Blvd., Culver City, CA 90230   310-397-8676
5945 Balboa Ave., San Diego, CA 92111   858-565-9181
46 Geary Street, San Francisco, CA 94108   415-781-5180

FLORIDA
145 S.W. 107th Ave., Miami, FL 33174   305-559-6715

HAWAII
1143 Bishop Street, Honolulu, HI 96813   808-521-2731
Neighbor Islands call: 800-259-8463

ILLINOIS
172 North Michigan Ave., Chicago, IL 60601   312-346-4228

LOUISIANA
4403 Veterans Memorial Blvd., Metairie, LA 70006   504-887-7631

MASSACHUSETTS
Rte. 1, 885 Providence Hwy., Dedham, MA 02026   781-326-5385

MISSOURI
9804 Watson Rd., St. Louis, MO 63126   314-965-3512

NEW JERSEY
561 U.S. Route 1, Wick Plaza, Edison, NJ 08817   732-572-1200

NEW YORK
150 East 52nd Street, New York, NY 10022   212-754-1110
78 Fort Place, Staten Island, NY 10301   718-447-5071

OHIO
2105 Ontario Street (at Prospect Ave.), Cleveland, OH 44115
 216-621-9427

PENNSYLVANIA
9171-A Roosevelt Blvd., Philadelphia, PA 19114; 215-676-9494

SOUTH CAROLINA
243 King Street, Charleston, SC 29401   843-577-0175

TENNESSEE
4811 Poplar Ave., Memphis, TN 38117   901-761-2987

TEXAS
114 Main Plaza, San Antonio, TX 78205   210-224-8101

VIRGINIA
1025 King Street, Alexandria, VA 22314   703-549-3806

CANADA
3022 Dufferin Street, Toronto, Ontario, Canada M6B 3T5
 416-781-9131
1155 Yonge Street, Toronto, Ontario, Canada M4T 1W2;
 416-934-3440

¡También somos su fuente para libros, videos y música en español!